After Marathon

WAR, SOCIETY AND MONEY
IN FIFTH–CENTURY GREECE

UTE WARTENBERG

D1363246

PUBLISHED FOR THE TRUSTEES OF THE BRITISH MUSEUM BY BRITISH MUSEUM PRESS

Acknowledgements

A number of people have considerably enhanced the content and appearance of this book. Jeremy Trevett discussed many of the historical problems, clarified many points and immeasurably improved my English text. I am indebted to Andrew Burnett, Selene Psoma, Andrew Meadows and Jonathan Williams for many helpful and encouraging comments. The photographs were shot by Chaz Howson, and Sarah Beyerl and Diana Delbridge helped with the preparation of the plates. My editor Colin Grant made sure that I did not forget the numerous tasks that needed to be done to complete this book and was ably assisted by designer Judy Cramond and copy-editor Michael Bird. Most of all I am indebted to Jeffrey Spier, who introduced me to many aspects of the subject and who, by reading the whole text, saved me from many errors. I am most grateful to all of them for their generous assistance.

Cover illustration: Head of Athena on a silver coin of Corinth. 1920.8.5.751
Title-Page illustration: Owl on an Athenian tetradrachm. 1949.4.11.427

Published by British Museum Press
A division of the British Museum Company Ltd
46 Bloomsbury Street, London WC1B 3QQ

British Library Cataloguing in Publication Data
A catalogue record for this book is available from the British Library

ISBN 0 7141 0882 0

Designed by Judy Cramond

Printed in Great Britain by
Henry Ling Ltd, The Dorset Press, Dorchester, Dorset

Contents

Introduction

Coins are rarely discussed in historical studies of Greece in the fifth century BC. This seems a peculiar phenomenon considering that money is of crucial importance to the understanding of the Athenian empire and the Peloponnesian War. After all, Athens received annual tribute payments from her allies, which were recorded on stone, and money plays a significant role in the account of the historian Thucydides. But how do the coins that survive from this period relate to the known financial information?

The need to organise an exhibition in the British Museum on the coins of Athens and her empire forced me to consider this problem. While doing some basic research, I discovered that the subject was not as easily accessible as I had expected. I therefore thought that it would be useful to have a short, general history on the use of money in the fifth century BC, and particularly during the period after the Persian Wars. The subjects chosen for discussion are highly selective, as I have not attempted to give an account of all the coinage of the period, the most notable omission being the regions of Italy and Sicily.

The book is divided into two parts: first a history and second a catalogue with descriptions and illustrations of 121 coins, which give an idea of the sort of coins produced during the period in question; with one exception they are all part of the collection of the British Museum. The illustrations in the first part of the book also come from the British Museum, and the number at the end of each caption refers either to the museum registration / catalogue number for the object concerned (all from the Coins and Medals Department except those preceded by 'GR' for the Department of Greek and Roman Antiquities) or to the 'no.' in the catalogue at the end of the book.

Design and Coinage

Modern states use coins, banknotes and stamps to display visual messages. These messages can vary from simple propaganda to something more subtle, with nuances of meaning which it is not always possible to understand. The new ten-pound note illustrates this point. First issued by the Bank of England in 1993, this note has on one side a portrait of Elizabeth II, on the other that of Charles Dickens, with his name and dates. Next to him is a depiction of a cricket match from one of his novels, *The Pickwick Papers*. If one wanted to illustrate a famous scene from Dickens, however, this might not be the obvious one to choose: how many people would recognise that the cricketing scene derives from Dickens's novel, were not both it and he labelled? More importantly, why was a cricket scene chosen for this banknote? Beyond its literary associations, this image has a wide appeal because it depicts a favourite national sport. But does this explain its presence on a banknote, or is this simply a case of a decision made by a passionate cricket fan in a crucial official position? The style of the note is also significant: the choice of a scene set in the Victorian era is enlightening about our own period, in which nostalgia and the evocation of so-called Victorian values have been of considerable political and social importance. What would an archaeologist in AD 3000 make of this artefact, if he had only a couple of modern paintings by Lucian Freud for comparison?

Drachm of Athens with the head of Athena in an Attic helmet on the obverse and an owl on the reverse.

no.65

The problem that the scholar faces when trying to interpret the coinage of Athens in the mid-fifth century BC is not dissimilar: the Parthenon sculptures and an Athenian drachm seem to represent different styles, although both were made at the same time. How are we to interpret the design of an Athenian coin (see illustration above)? On the obverse is a head

The sandal that the hero Jason lost in a river is depicted on the reverse of this coin of Larissa, with the head of a young man on the obverse.

1885.4.4.2

sorts were popular, and generally only one side, usually the obverse, had an image. Some of these designs were a pun on the city's name – coins of Melos depicted an apple (*melos* is the Greek word for apple). The corn ear of Metapontum, the silphium plant of Cyrene and the turtle of Aegina were well-known symbols of their cities. In the late sixth century the habit of representing a deity or religious symbol on coins became popular, and this remained a feature of coinage for many centuries to come. Such emblems, often associated with one of the principal deities, helped to define a city's identity and set it apart from other cities, which may have been long-standing rivals. This helps to explain why coin designs rarely changed, and why changes may have had a religious or political significance. Sometimes we know little about the authority that issued particular coins and have to interpret the images on them in the light of other designs.

Religious or mythological images were often associated with local myths, some of which were well-known throughout the Greek world, although many were of purely local significance. Athena can be seen on the coins of Corinth, in combination with the famous mythical winged horse Pegasus, who was tamed by the Corinthian hero Bellerophon. The coinage of Thebes, which has a Boeotian shield on the obverse, illustrates various deeds of Heracles. A sandal on a coin of Larissa alludes to a local myth about Jason. In the story, Pelias, King of Iolkos, had been warned by a mysterious oracle that he would be killed by a man wearing one sandal. When Jason appeared one day before the king, wearing just one sandal, Pelias tried to escape his fate by sending him off on the famous quest for the Golden Fleece, in the hope he would never return.

Heracles was a popular motif on Greek coins and is depicted on the reverse of this Boeotian example, with the Boeotian shield on the obverse.
BMC 49

Somewhat different in kind are the designs that were common on coins of northern Greece. Those of the Macedonian city of Akanthos show a remarkable image of a lion attacking a bull. This carefully composed scene was evidently popular, judging by the variations on it that can be found on coins of neighbouring Stageira or of Skione, where the bull is replaced by a boar or stag. The griffin on the coinage of Abdera, which was adopted from the coins of Teos (the city that had founded Abdera as a colony), and the Gorgon's head of Neapolis had close parallels in coin designs from Asia Minor.

Many of the images on Macedonian coins show a surprising degree of movement, unlike the static designs of the Greek mainland. One of the most vivid and popular images, found on a large number of coinages, shows a satyr carrying away a nymph. But not all Macedonian coins depict scenes of such violence: the image of a satyr running away with an amphora displays a lively wit, far from the stern seriousness of the face of Athena on Athenian coins. Unparalleled in its charm is the attractive coin of an as yet unknown mint on which two maenads (female followers of the god Dionysos) are lifting a heavy amphora. The prominence of wine and its patron god on these coins probably alludes to the importance of viniculture in the society and economy of the region.

Another feature, which made its début on coinage of the Classical period (500-323 BC) is the custom of putting the image of a ruler on a coin. To this day portraits of the head of state are used to symbolise the authority of the state. This phenomenon, which originated in the first coins of the Persian satraps (provincial governors) of the late fifth century BC, became common in the Hellenistic period. No independent

Below left: Animal fights, here between a lion and stag on a coin of Stageira, Macedonia, are a common feature of Archaic art.
no.15

Below: The city of Abdera used the same griffin design as her mother-city Teos.
BMC 33

Above: The Persian king holds a spear and a bow to indicate his military stature. BMC 74

Above: This bearded man with a soft cap is often thought to represent the satrap Tissaphernes. no.96

Greek city-state adopted this style, however, even when ruled by an individual, although it is common on coins of cities under Persian influence. The Persian king is depicted on many Achaemenid coins, a custom which is easily understood in the context of Achaemenid monuments, where he and his various symbols of power are frequently represented. Coins showing him running with a spear and a dagger emphasise his role as the military leader of the Persian empire.

The famous tetradrachm (illustrated below left) that is said to bear the portrait of the Persian satrap Tissaphernes is strongly influenced by Greek style. While intended to present an image of the satrap, as is shown by the peculiar headgear which indicates his status, the portrait is not necessarily realistic. It may be compared with a small bronze coin (no. 97) depicting a bearded head of a man and inscribed with the letters ΤΙΣΣΑ, which identify the man as Tissaphernes. It is hard to detect any resemblance between the two images, although it could be argued that the earlier coin depicts a younger man, and it seems more likely that the two designs represent Tissaphernes in two different roles (it is difficult, however, to say what new role Tissaphernes might have taken on in the first few years of the fourth century, when the small bronze coin was minted).

The interpretation of coin images is, as in the last example, sometimes made easier by inscriptions accompanying the design. The most common inscription is that of the name of the city, or, more specifically, its inhabitants (e.g. 'of the Syracusans'). Such inscriptions may be abbreviated to a few letters (in Athens, ΑΘΕ) or just one, as in the case of Corinth, which used the Archaic Greek letter *koppa*. Sometimes an artist's signature appears, but we normally know nothing beyond his name. In a few cases inscriptions clarify images which would otherwise have been obscure even to contemporaries. Sometimes it was even felt necessary to explain what the nature of the round piece of silver was: on coins of the Thracian rulers Seuthes I and Getas we find several different versions of the Greek word for 'coin' and the ruler's name.

Trade

Because of the greatness of our city, there is an influx of all manner of goods from throughout the world, with the result that the enjoyment of domestic produce is no more familiar to us than foreign goods.

THUCYDIDES, *History of the Peloponnesian War*, II, XXXVIII, 2

It is easy to exaggerate the importance of coins for Greek trade in the Classical period. Obviously they served as units of exchange, but trade could operate perfectly well without them. After all, long-distance trade had flourished in the Greek world for many centuries before the introduction of coinage. Coins had both advantages and disadvantages for trade, as we shall see. Moreover, Greek states tended, with certain exceptions, to take little interest in commerce, considering it an area best left to private enterprise. Since coins were issued by the civic authorities, it is unlikely that their primary purpose was to facilitate trade. Coinage certainly had some role in trade, but its exact function is not easy to determine.

By the middle of the sixth century BC coins had acquired the familiar form of a stamped piece of metal of standard weight. Since early coins presumably had the same value as the weight of bullion of which they were composed, why were they made? Minting is an expensive process, in which dies have to be cut, the metal weighed and prepared for striking, and the staff of the mint paid, and city-states must therefore have had good reasons for making coins when they did. Presumably the most common reasons related to an 'internal market': to make payment and purchases on behalf of the city. Thus, insofar as coins were minted to fulfil a commercial purpose, it was to facilitate exchange within a city, and thereby benefit its citizens. What subsequent use was made of them, for example in trade beyond the city's territory, was in most cases beyond the state authority's interest or control.

Most economic activity in Archaic Greece was geared towards an ideal of self-sufficiency: the individual household or community sought to produce all that it needed to survive. Such commodities as oil, grain and wine were produced for consumption, without the direct intention of creating a surplus to sell to others. Yet seaborne trade certainly took place during this period. We have numerous references to traders sailing around the Mediterranean. At the beginning of the sixth century the poet Solon referred to a class of people who travelled by sea and made money by trading goods; even earlier, Hesiod's father is said to have made his living from trade. In reality, all manner of goods were traded: corn, wine, pottery, oriental luxuries and precious metals. This last is important – both bullion and jewellery were objects of trade long before coinage began.

The kinds of goods that could have been bought by a rich Athenian in Classical Athens are listed in a passage from a lost work of the satirical poet Hermippos:

Coin of Cyrene, which was famous for its plantations of silphium, a plant used for medical and culinary purposes.

no.121

from Cyrene silphium stalks and oxhides, from the Hellespont tunny and smoked fish, from Italy salt and ribs of beef, Syracuse offers port and cheese ... from Egypt sailcloth and raw materials for ropes, from Syria frankincense. Fair Crete sends cypress wood for the gods, Libya plentiful ivory to buy, and Rhodes raisins and figs sweet as dreams; from Euboea come pears and big apples, slaves without tattoos; and from the Paphlagonians dates that come from Zeus and shiny almonds ... Phoenicia supplies the fruit of the date-palm and fine wheat-flour, Carthage rugs and cushions of many colours.

This list of luxury goods nicely illustrates Thucydides' comment quoted at the beginning of this chapter. Although we have no evidence as to their prices, some idea of these can be gained from an inscription that lists the confiscated property of the men who were said

to have mutilated the herms in Athens in 415, just before the
Athenian fleet set out for Sicily. The men who were condemned
for this sacrilege belonged to the Athenian upper classes, and
the property that was taken included estates, animals and
slaves. The average price for a slave was 170-180 drachms, but
certain categories of slaves, such as a Carian goldsmith (360
drachms) or a Macedonian woman (310 drachms), were much
dearer than others. Prices of pottery in the fifth century are
sometimes preserved on the vases themselves, on the bottoms
of which a figure may be written. A decorated *lekythion* (a small
perfume bottle) would have cost roughly three-quarters of an
obol (6 obols = 1 drachm), with prices for larger vases such as
decorated amphorae rising to 8-10 obols.

Coinage had a greater impact at the local level. In the
late fifth century, and still more in the fourth, we are well
informed about the economy of Athens, with its flourishing
market, the Agora, and its harbour town at Piraeus. By the end
of the fifth century coins were used by ordinary citizens to buy
goods, and people commonly borrowed coined money from
each other. Small obols changed hands, and in southern Italy
bronze coins circulated (being of much lower value, they were
more suitable for day-to-day transactions); these soon became
common in mainland Greece as well.

Most Archaic and early Classical coins were probably of
too high a denomination to have played a role in everyday
transactions, and they were more likely to have been used for

Hoards from the Near East
often contain coins which
have been cut to check for
their metal content, like
this Archaic example from
Athens.
1929.5.1.12

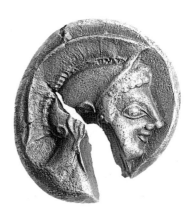

overseas trade. This hypothesis is supported by the fact that most of these large coins were found in areas with which the Greeks traded, especially in Egypt and the Near East. Hoards from these areas, however, appear to have been assembled because of their silver content and not for their monetary value as coins, since they include cut coins, fragments of coins, pieces of silver, jewellery and ingots, all mixed together. Such heterogeneous collections may have been associated with trade with Egypt and the east, although firm evidence for this is lacking.

Coins from northern Greece, Athens, the Aegean and Persia are well represented in these hoards. By contrast, those from the Peloponnese, Sicily and southern Italy are rare, tending to be found closer to their place of issue, in hoards which are generally much smaller and contain mainly local coinage. It is surprising that Athenian 'owls' are not found even more frequently than they are, considering their wide use in the fifth century. This may be because many of them were melted down and reminted in cities which were short of silver bullion, such as Corinth. It is particularly striking that coins from the Thraco-Macedonian area are found in the Near East, and this phenomenon requires closer examination. The most important such coinages are those of Akanthos, Abdera, Thasos and the Bisaltae. High-denomination coins of Akanthos, in particular, seem to have circulated very widely, occurring in hoards from Sicily, Egypt, the Near East, Afghanistan and even further afield. The case of Akanthos is particularly interesting. We know that

Coin of Maroneia with a vine on the reverse and a horse on the obverse. Wine was an important export for many Thracian cities. BMC 27

the city was agriculturally rich, and the importance of wine for this area is clear. Thucydides reports that the Akanthians surrendered to the Spartan general Brasidas in 424 because they feared he would destroy their crop. The mines from which the Akanthians obtained their silver were also near, and later evidence points to a trade in salt. Evidently Akanthos had rich resources, but it is unclear on what their massive silver coinage was spent, or why it was minted.

The coins of Akanthos are found in Egypt and were certainly used in trade with the Near East, although it does not follow that its citizens were buying goods from the western provinces of the Persian empire. These regions provided all sorts of luxury goods – spices, papyrus, linen, glass and perfumes – and Egypt was throughout its history a major source of grain. The island of Kythera, which lies off the Peloponnese, was a landing place for ships arriving from Egypt and Libya. In addition, Arabia produced ivory; copper came from Cyprus; the Black Sea area supplied much of the grain that Athens needed, and was also rich in fish. Many of these commodities were doubtless bought with Greek silver, although the Egyptians at least had no *monetary* use for Greek coins as such. The gap in the evidence is obvious: we know that large coinages were produced by Greek cities and we find Greek coins in Egypt but we do not know why and how they ended up there.

Nevertheless, within the Greek world coins became increasingly used as an easily portable medium of exchange. Other things being equal, it was more convenient to have a talent of silver in coin rather than bullion. Moreover, certain coins were almost universally accepted, and were regarded as desirable because of their generally high quality and reliable metal content. Such were the coins of Aegina, Kyzikos and, above all, Athens. Just as the American dollar is nowadays accepted worldwide as 'hard currency', the Athenian 'owls' could be used throughout the Mediterranean world. A corollary of this was that coins from small or remote cities were often regarded with suspicion. Many ancient coins of this period have been cut, in order to test their silver content. Money-changers were to be found in most Greek harbours and markets, but they charged for their services. Consequently, many coins had little currency outside the city that issued them, even if they were of unimpeachable metallic purity.

If we now turn to local trade and markets in the Classical city, we face difficulties which arise from a lack of numismatic evidence. Until relatively recently, both scholars of Greek numismatics and archaeologists were primarily concerned with the study and collecting of large silver coins, and few paid much attention to small silver or bronze pieces. Such coins are consistently under-represented in the archaeological record, and the standard books on Greek coinage leave the reader with the impression that most Classical coins were beautiful tetradrachms! Fortunately things are slowly changing, and more emphasis is now put on silver fractions. A highly significant body of material, consisting of more than 16,000 coins found in the excavations of the Athenian Agora, has recently been published and is helping to show how this important market-place worked. Although only eighty-four of them date from the Archaic and Classical periods and are therefore relevant for our purposes, they are of considerable interest. As one would expect, the overwhelming majority of coins that can be dated to the sixth or fifth centuries (sixty-nine) are from Athens. When distributed by date the following picture emerges: there are eight coins of the so-called *Wappenmünzen*, the Athenian series that preceded the 'owls'; the denominations represented are three obols, four drachms and one didrachm. What is surprising is the number of these coins found, since they are generally considered rather rare. Although even an obol represented a relatively high value, one can assume that these coins were used in transactions in the Agora, even if not for the purchase of daily food.

The 'owl' coins that were found in the Agora belong, with two exceptions (an obol and a tetradrachm of the unwreathed variety of *c.*510-500), to the large group of crude 'owls', the so-called standardised group (see p. 7), which were probably minted from the 450s onwards. A good range of denominations is represented in these finds: eleven tetradrachms (three of them plated), fourteen drachms (one plated), thirteen diobols, one trihemiobol (one-and-a-half obols), seventeen obols and three hemiobols. These show that the Athenian economy became more monetised in the second half of the fifth century, an impression strongly supported by literary sources. The foreign silver coins found on the Agora are from Aegina (five staters, among them a plated coin), Kyzikos (one electrum stater), Siphnos (one plated forgery) and Persia (one gold daric of *c.* 500 BC). Apart from the Archaic coin of Siphnos, all these were major international currencies, and the find of the gold and electrum coins shows that these valuable pieces were used in Athens.

The large number of small coins found in the Athenian Agora serves as a reminder that silver fractions were much more common than is generally assumed. Often a single hoard of fractions can completely change our picture of the sizes of these coinages. They need to be collected more systematically, although the nature of small coinage makes it less likely to have been buried in hoards.

One can conclude that coins were certainly used for some daily purchases in a city such as Athens and that this practice became more widespread towards the end of the fifth century. However, the fact that large parts of Greece remained without small coinage, or any coins at all, indicates that coinage was not essential for a market economy. The large number of coins from the Hellenistic period found in the Athenian Agora serves as a reminder of how unusual coinage in general was in the preceding Classical period and how much it was to develop in later centuries.

Athens and her Empire

When the Greeks claimed victory over the Persians in 479 BC on the battlefield of Plataea, it was by no means certain that the Persians would not attack again. It was decided to form an alliance against them, and the Athenians, who had the largest fleet, were the obvious leaders if the fight were to be taken to the Persians and the Greek islands protected. The psychological impact of the Persian invasion had been profound, especially for the Athenians, who in 480 were forced to evacuate Athens and abandon the Acropolis and its temples to the enemy. The victory over the Persians was seen as the triumph of Greek discipline and the maintenance of the freedom of the whole of Greece from barbarian rule. The *Histories* of Herodotus, who chose the Persian Wars as his central subject, and the tragedies of Aeschylus draw a sharp contrast between Greeks and barbarians. This is also reflected in the sculptures of the Parthenon, where the depiction of the mythical battle between the man-like Lapiths and bestial centaurs was surely intended to echo the triumph of Greeks over Persians.

The evidence provided by coins, however, undermines the schematic distinction which the Greeks drew between themselves and 'barbarians'. Indeed, the origin of coinage lies in 'barbarian' Lydia, whence it spread to the Greek cities, and some non-Greek areas, of Asia Minor, and thence to the rest of the Mediterranean world. The feature that unites coins of Corinth or Athens with those from places as distant as Cyrene in North Africa or Persia, however, is their distinctively Greek style, and many can be considered as great works of Greek miniature art. Furthermore, they circulated beyond the boundaries of the Greek world, as far as the Black Sea, Egypt, Persia and Afghanistan.

The alliance that was formed against the Persians after the war was initially a small organisation of Greeks from Ionia, Aeolia and elsewhere, under the leadership of Athens. The temple of Apollo on the sacred island of Delos was chosen as the site for its treasury and its regular meetings – hence modern scholars refer to it as the Delian League. Membership varied from time to time, but there were usually between 140 and 180 members. In all, over 230 different cities belonged at some point in the League's existence. All member states contributed either ships or money. Gradually the League turned into an Athenian empire: in 454 its administration was transferred from Delos to Athens, and there was a move away from contributing ships to money, which the Athenians encouraged. These payments, which can be seen as a form of tribute, were ruthlessly extorted by the Athenians from their erstwhile allies, now subjects.

Many powerful ancient states derived much of their income from tribute paid by subject peoples. The most successful example of this in the Classical period was the Persian empire, ruled by a king. To facilitate its administration, this vast empire was divided into twenty smaller units, which were governed by satraps. If we can believe Herodotus (III, 89-96), these districts together contributed a total of 14,560 Euboean talents. Some of this was paid in coined money, but the majority of the contributions were made in bullion or other commodities. A smaller empire like that of Seuthes, the king of the Thracian Odrysae in the late fifth century, is said to have raised 400 talents in gold and silver, and the same amount again in gifts (Thucydides, II, 97). The total tribute raised from the Athenian empire is difficult to assess, since it fluctuated from year to year: Thucydides gives 600 talents, whereas the epigraphic accounts suggest a lower figure (probably only 430 talents in 431 BC).

We are relatively well informed about individual tribute payments because one-sixtieth of each state's contribution was donated to the treasury of Athena at Athens, and epigraphical records of many of these donations have survived. The amounts of money paid by member states varied sharply, ranging from 100 drachms to 30 talents (1 talent = 6,000 drachms). The following is a list of the major payers, with comments on their coinage.

IONIA The biggest contributor in Ionia was Kyme, which paid 9 talents in 441. It is noteworthy that this city had a minute coin production, consisting of obols with an eagle head, which was doubtless not minted for tribute payments. Other states which paid heavily are Erythrai, Ephesos, Teos and Miletos, which in the same year paid between 7 and 5 talents each. All of them minted coins in the fifth century, though not on the same scale as the island states of Samos, Chios or Lesbos, which were allies of Athens but contributed ships.

BLACK SEA COLONIES Further north, in the Black Sea district, we should note the contrast between the important cities of Byzantion and Kyzikos. Byzantion, ideally sited for trade on the Bosporus, paid over 15 talents but did not issue its own coinage. Kyzikos contributed 9 talents, but its coinage, consisting of the so-called Kyzicene staters made of electrum, circulated widely and were extremely popular in mainland Greece. Unlike other Greek coins, these carry a variety of beautiful designs, to which a tunny fish is added as the city badge. Other major contributors in the region were Perinthos (which issued no coinage), Lampsakos, Chalkedon and Selymbria.

Coin of Phaselis, in south-west Asia Minor, which issued silver coins in the fifth century BC.

no.115

SOUTH-WEST ASIA MINOR This was a non-Greek area with some Greek settlements, and its largest single contribution came from the Lycians. In the tribute list of 445 they paid 10 talents, but payments seem to have stopped by 440. In the 420s the Athenians sent ships to try to collect tribute, but without much success. This was an area which Athens sought to exploit, but over which their control was tenuous. That it was a potentially rich source of tribute is suggested by the large number of Lycian coins of the fifth century. These have various designs, and in some cases the names of rulers. Among the Greek cities,

Kamiros, Lindos and Ialysos, all on the island of Rhodes, paid up to 9 talents. These cities issued their own coinage in the Archaic and Classical periods.

AEGEAN ISLANDS Among the Aegean islands the largest sum (30 talents) was paid by Aegina, just south-west of Athens. Aegina had been the first city in mainland Greece to produce silver coins. Initially an ally of Sparta, Aegina came under Athenian control in the early 450s. There is no evidence, however, that coin production stopped for more than a few years. Other major contributors in this region include Paros, Naxos, Andros, Karystos and Keos. Naxos, Keos and Andros issued coins in the Archaic period, but no coins are known from the time of Athenian domination. Paros issued a series of coins, which consists mainly of drachms.

NORTHERN GREECE In the north the largest payments were made by Thasos, Abdera, Ainos, Argilos, Potidaia, Skione, Terone, Samothrace, Akanthos, Aineia and Peparethos. All the cities in this area issued coins, often in large quantities (see pp. 22-4).

This Archaic coin of Terone was buried in a hoard in Egypt in c. 500 BC along with many other coins from northern Greece. 1929.5.1.4

There is no doubt that the cities which paid most tribute were the richest. But it emerges that there was no necessary connection between wealth and the issuing of coins. Although a few of the largest contributors minted their own, their coinages were often small (both in volume and size of denominations), and some large payers such as Byzantion and Perinthos did not mint at all; presumably they paid their tribute in coins which were issued elsewhere, or in bullion. Byzantion, for example, which grew rich from the lucrative Black Sea trade, may have collected much coined money from harbour dues and the like. It should be noted that there are fewer cities minting in this period, for example, in the Aegean than in the period before the Persian Wars. Nevertheless, it must be allowed that some of the coinage of subject states was used to pay tribute to Athens. But what was the effect of the Athenian empire on these coinages? To examine this more closely, let us look at Macedonia and Thrace, areas rich in precious metals, which have been the subject of much recent numismatic interest.

The coins of the northern region fall into three main categories. First, from the beginning of the fifth century, large-denomination coins were issued by tribes such as the Deronnes, Ichnae, Orescii and Edones, whose king Getas issued coins in his own name. Some of these continued until *c.* 470 BC, by which time they had been joined by those of the Bisaltae. Second, coins were issued by kings of Macedonia. Herodotus reports that in 480 Alexander I obtained control of a silver mine near Lake Prasias, from which he earned the impressive sum of one talent a day. However, the earliest coins of Alexander I, the first king to issue coinage, resemble those of the Bisaltae, but seem to be less numerous. Alexander's coins may have been minted from 470 BC or possibly later, as his main minting activities seem to decline after 460 towards the end of his reign. The Bisaltae stopped issuing coins in this decade, perhaps because they lost control of their mines. In any case, control of resources was clearly crucial. Perdikkas, who came to the throne after Alexander's violent death and reigned until 413, lost the mines, and his coinage and that of his successor Archelaos (413-399) are of only small denominations. Various Thracian rulers also issued their own coinage, of whom the best known is Seuthes, who became king of the Odrysian kingdom in 424.

The third group of northern Greek coins are those of the cities founded on the coast of Macedonia and Thrace. The first to mint their own coins were Abdera, Akanthos, Mende, Neapolis, Dikaia, Skione, Thasos and an uncertain city ('Lete'), which can all be dated to the sixth century. They are followed by another group of coins from the first two decades of the fifth century: Aigai, Aineia, Sermylia, Peparethos, Potidaia and Terone. In addition, we have many coins from this area which (in the absence of an inscription) cannot be attributed to any particular city (see no. 25). Attribution is made harder by the fact

that many designs resemble each other, although new
discoveries continue to lead to advances. Thus it has recently
been shown by Katerini Liampi that the city of Argilos minted
an extensive series of silver coins. Argilos was of considerable
importance in the Archaic and early Classical periods, but
declined when Amphipolis was founded nearby in 437/6 by
Athens. Its extensive coinage demonstrates its earlier wealth.
The coins, which appear in a number of hoards, were probably
issued between 500 and 480 BC.

Technical numismatic arguments confirm the impression
that northern Greek cities issued coins in massive quantities
during the fifth century. Scholars have been compiling die-
studies for the last hundred years, in which they attempt to
collect every surviving specimen of a particular series. All coins
are identified according to the obverse and reverse dies
employed, and the number of obverse dies that were used for a
particular series is generally considered a reasonable indicator of
its total volume. New coins that are found can usually be
inserted into these series, because they are from known dies or,
when from new dies, are related in some way to the existing
corpus of dies. Such studies have been done for a number of
important coinages, but some appear to be more conclusive than
others. Thus the number of subsequently discovered dies
needing to be added to E. Boehringer's analysis of the coinage of
Syracuse is relatively small in comparison to those not included
in J.F.M. May's works on Abdera; not only new dies but coins of
completely new designs from these cities continue to be
discovered, many of which are unique. This seems to indicate
that very large numbers of coins were minted in both
Macedonia and Thrace. The fact that many are known
only by unique examples suggests that large quantities
were melted down, some no doubt at Athens, others by
states which had no silver of their own. Coins of
Syracuse tended to circulate locally, and the wars that
affected Sicily in the fifth century led wealthy Sicilians
to hide their money by burying it in the ground; some of

Coin of the powerful
Bisaltae tribe, who
produced a large and
impressive silver coinage.
no.4

these 'hoards' were never recovered by their owners, and have been found in recent times. The rareness of such hoards in northern Greece means that our knowledge of the coins of this area is comparatively deficient.

The tribute raised from the north was clearly important to Athens. In 446, a year for which the records are quite complete, the region of Thrace contributed the largest share – 120 talents out of a total of 417. These figures translate into a massive quantity of coins, since each talent consisted of 1,500 tetradrachms. Much of the silver of the area was turned into coins and paid to Athens. How did the Athenian empire affect the coinages of the north? Surprisingly little, it seems, at least to start with. The Greek cities minted some coins specifically in order to pay tribute, but it must be remembered that great numbers of coins were being issued long before Athenian control was established. Moreover, not all coin-issuing cities were early members of the League. The most prominent example is Akanthos, with its very large coinage, which appears only in 445 BC in the tribute lists (it may have been contributing ships before, or may have not joined the League at all). Specific Athenian influence is hard to detect on any of these coins. The fact that some of the cities (e.g. Akanthos, Potidaia) apparently used the Attic weight standard is not necessarily relevant, since it is difficult to distinguish this from the Euboean standard (many of the Greek cities of the area were colonies of Euboea).

What is significant, however, is the change in weight standard from Attic to Thraco-Macedonian in the coinage of Akanthos. It is tempting to attribute this to the activities of the Spartan general Brasidas, who in 424 captured the cities of Akanthos, Stageira, Argilos on the Chalcidian peninsula, and the Athenian colony of Amphipolis. The Athenians, who had imposed heavy tributes on their allies in 425, were unpopular (and the Macedonian king Perdikkas was also trying to weaken their influence). Brasidas then moved against Terone, another major ally of Athens, and Skione and Mende also revolted. Athens re-established control at these two cities, but Amphipolis remained in revolt. The change away from the Attic weight standard at Akanthos surely has a political significance, and may well have been highly topical, as we shall now see.

Numerous Athenian decrees relate to tribute. One stipulates the appointment of collectors in the cities of the empire, who are to be personally responsible for the tribute (Meiggs, Lewis 68). Another, of disputed date, seeks to tighten up tribute payments by introducing various enforcement measures (Meiggs, Lewis 46). But the most interesting for our purposes is the so-called Coinage Decree. Both its content and its date are contentious, but recent epigraphic and hoard evidence tends in the same direction. The text of the law, which survives in eight fragments from different places in the empire, is not fully preserved, but it clearly bans the use of any non-Athenian silver coins in cities of the empire and requires everyone to use Athenian currency. The mint at Athens is to replace foreign with Athenian coins for a fee. The following sentence, which is well-preserved, was added to the oath that Athenian councillors had to take: 'If anyone strikes silver coins in the cities and does not use Athenian coins or weights or measures but foreign coins or weights or measures, I shall punish him and fine him according to the previous decree that Klearchos proposed.' The decree was to be set up in the market-place of the cities; the fact that fragments have been found in Syme, Aphytis, Cos, Siphnos, Smyrna, Odessa and Hamaxitos illustrates that at least this part of the decree was carried out.

How far the minting of silver coins by the allied cities did in fact cease has been a matter of debate ever since the first fragments of the Coinage Decree were discovered. The main problem is that, like most Athenian decrees of the fifth century, this decree was undated. Greek inscriptions can in general be dated by the letter forms used, and in this case the number of bars of the letter *sigma* on one of the fragments has been thought to show that the decree was inscribed no later than 445; it has customarily been dated to the early 440s, just after Athens moved the League treasury from Delos to Athens. For a long time this date was treated by scholars as a fixed point, to which any interruption in the subject cities' coinages was to be referred.

There has always been opposition, however, to this dating of the Coinage Decree, with a date in the 420s also having its supporters. One of the strongest arguments in favour of a later date is a famous passage in the *Birds*, a comedy by Aristophanes of 414 BC. In Cloudcuckooland, an imaginary new city, a decree-seller arrives who is trying to sell his wares. On offer is a decree that 'All citizens of Cloudcuckooland are to employ the same weights, measures and decrees as the Olophyxians [the inhabitants of a small town on the Mount Athos peninsula]'. Even before any of the fragments of the Coinage Decree were discovered, the classical scholar Ulrich von Wilamowitz-Moellendorff had seen in this passage a reference to a lost Athenian decree that required the allies to use the same coins, weights and measures. When the decree was found, a date in the late 420s or early 410s seemed to be implied by Aristophanes, especially as his comedies tend to be topical. A further argument for a late date is the fact that two copies of the Decree were discovered in cities that became allies later than 440: Syme first appears on the tribute lists in 433, whilst Hamaxitos in the Troad came under Athenian control only after 427. In addition, many epigraphists now doubt that the argument regarding letter style is correct, and one document previously regarded as 'pre-445' is now dated to 418/417 (Meiggs, Lewis 37). A strong case can thus be made for dating the Coinage Decree in the 420s, a period in which the Athenians pursued harsh imperialist policies under the influence of the demagogue Kleon. The unusually high assessment of tribute in 425 (1,460 talents were demanded) captures the mood of the time. Athens, at war with the cities of the Peloponnesian League was financially vulnerable, and these measures were meant to ease the pain.

Assuming the Coinage Decree belongs to the 420s, how successful was it? Previously scholars have looked for possible interruptions of allied coinages in the mid-fifth century, but what of the numismatic evidence for the late 420s? One feature of the period is the growing prominence of Athenian coinage as an international currency; these were the coins in which everyone wanted to be paid – even Athens' enemies! When the Persian satrap Tissaphernes asked for Spartan military help in Ionia, he promised to pay the Spartan expenses for a fleet, and in the winter of 412/11 he paid 'one Attic drachm a day to each man; for the future he wanted to pay half a drachm until he had asked the king for permission to pay the full drachm' (Thucydides, VIII, 29). It seems possible that Tissaphernes minted imitation Athenian coins for this purpose, and it may have been then that he issued the famous tetradrachm with his own image (see p. 10). After the end of the Peloponnesian War (431-404 BC), when the availability of Athenian coins in the east seems to decline, imitation coins were frequently minted in order to meet the demand for them. For example, large numbers of Athenian 'owls', which until recently were regarded as of genuine Athenian issue, seem to have been minted in Egypt.

If we return to the Coinage Decree, it is hard to demonstrate that it had much effect, particularly since it was in force for less than two decades before the collapse of Athens. The Athenians may have found it difficult to enforce, given their other military preoccupations. Why was it passed? The economic arguments for a unified coinage are obvious, as it made commercial transactions much easier. Equally persuasive is the suggestion that it was introduced for the Athenians' own convenience, since the administration of the empire, and in particular the maintenance of their fleet, which became increasingly critical during the Peloponnesian War, involved many purchases and payments, all of which would now be made in a single and familiar currency. Moreover, the Athenians may have hoped to make money from the fees charged for reminting coins as 'owls'. The imposition of such a regulation, to be prominently displayed in every subject state, was a graphic reminder of Athenian dominance, imposed by the fleet which was paid for by the silver extracted from the allies.

This Persian coin represents a fascinating combination of the famous Athenian owl and an inscription referring to the Persian king.
no.96

Greece at War

The effects of war on coinage in the fifth century BC are difficult to assess. From the designs employed on the coins of the period one could easily gain the impression that its impact was minimal, and that the Greeks continued to be mainly preoccupied with religion and myth. It is rare to find direct allusions to contemporary events on coins or vases, and the great wars of the Classical age are no exception.

The unsuccessful Persian attempt to conquer mainland Greece at the beginning of the fifth century is narrated by Herodotus. He sometimes refers to money and financial matters in his account of the Persian Wars, but he does not establish a direct causal connection between them and the events he describes. By the time Thucydides composed his *History of the Peloponnesian War,* however, at the end of the fifth century, the situation had changed completely, and we can detect in his writing considerable interest in wealth and money as explanatory concepts. His story is one in which money and monetary economies are crucial factors, and many Athenian military operations are attributed to Athens' regional economic interests. A similar attention to financial detail can be seen in the inscriptions that survive from the period. These include inventories of temples and accounts for building work and military campaigns, and show how money was raised, stored and spent. In some cases we find references to actual coins rather than to sums of money, but a direct connection between the surviving coins and the events of war is not always clear.

War is expensive and wealth essential for victory. As Cicero said, 'unlimited money is the sinews of war'. But in the ancient world such wealth did not necessarily take the form of coined money. This point is clearly illustrated by a famous

Red-figure vase showing a Persian soldier with a bow and a Greek warrior leading a horse.
GR Vase E253

inscribed stele, usually dated to the early years of the Peloponnesian War (Meiggs, Lewis 67). This was found in Sparta and records contributions to the Spartans from various of their supporters, not only such states as Melos and Ephesos but also individuals. Some payments are in coin (Aeginetan staters and darics), but others are in food (corn and even raisins). This list indicates both the diversity of contributions to the Spartan war fund, and the fact that coinage was not essential for waging war.

Nevertheless, in the fifth century coined money became increasingly important for the waging of war, and in particular naval war. In the opening pages of his history, Thucydides describes the rise of ancient states, attributing this to their possession of accumulated wealth and sea-power. In so doing, he reflects the realities of his own day. A navy was expensive: timber had to be procured, often from distant regions, shipbuilders paid, sailcloth bought and rowers hired. In the early fifth century new techniques for building both warships and merchant ships were developed. This modern technology was expensive, and it was Athens that took advantage of it. In the mid-480s an exceptionally rich vein was struck in the silver mines of Laurion, and it was initially proposed that each Athenian citizen should receive a bonanza of ten drachms. But then, as Herodotus reports (VII, 144), 'Themistocles persuaded the Athenians to make no such division, but out of the money to build two hundred ships for the war, that is for the war with Aegina.' Thus the Athenians became seamen, and their fleet made a vital contribution to the Greek defeat of the Persians in 480 at the Battle of Salamis. As a result of this victory, Athens became the dominant naval power of Greece.

Naval war was fundamentally different from that on land, being both more time-consuming and much more expensive. In land warfare, citizens served for a short period only, usually a few weeks or even days, and provided their own arms and armour; war was rarely allowed to disrupt the harvest, which was vital to both sides. Naval expeditions, on the other hand, could last much longer, since their targets were often distant, and rowers had to be compensated for the consequent loss of income. But the money devoted to the fleet was well spent: it enabled Athens to build and control her empire, since even distant members could be easily reached and the payment of tribute enforced. This tribute in turn enabled Athens to enlarge her fleet and increase her power. The Athenians presumably met many of their naval expenses in coined money, and the large numbers of coins struck during the fifth century were doubtless spent mainly on the fleet. The fleet was also used to import grain from the Black Sea area, on which the Athenian population depended.

Other military expenses are referred to by Thucydides, not least the vast amounts of money expended on sieges, for some of which we are given precise costs. Apart from the large numbers of men involved in such operations, all sorts of siege machines were needed. The revolt of the island of Thasos in 465-3, however, ended with a financial gain for the Athenians, as they required the Thasians to repay the costs of the three-year siege and made them liable for tribute in the future. Similarly, the revolt of the island of Samos, which lasted from 441 to 439, cost at least 1,200 talents to suppress. The Samians were required to pay back this sum over the following years. And at the beginning of the Peloponnesian War the Athenians expended large sums when they besieged Potidaia. This city in the peninsula of the Chalcidice was a colony of Corinth, and had been one of the major contributors of tribute in the Athenian empire. In 433 relations between Athens and Corinth worsened, and the Athenians tried to pre-empt a revolt in Potidaia by

This famous inscription commemorates the Athenians who fell in 432 BC before the town of Potidaia.

GR Inscriptions 37

applying military pressure to the inhabitants; they initially sent a force of thirty ships and 1,000 hoplites (heavily armed foot-soldiers), which was soon enlarged by forty more ships and another 2000 hoplites under the Athenian general Kallias. The siege lasted two and a half years, until the winter of 430/29, when the Potidaians gave in and accepted the Athenian terms to leave the city. Thucydides says that the siege cost 2,000 talents. In return, the Athenians settled some of their own people in Potidaian territory. In other sieges we know that male citizens were often killed, and women and children sold as slaves, which ensured some recompense for the successful besiegers.

One reason why Athens spent so much money dealing with these rebellious allies was that they controlled important sources of revenue. Thasos and Potidaia grew rich from trade and mining. Samos was also commercially important, and Byzantion, which revolted at the same time, dominated the trade route to the Black Sea.

Another cost of war was the pay of sailors in the fleet. Thucydides says that 60 talents of uncoined silver was worth a month's pay for sixty ships, and that sailors were paid one drachm a day. Rowers and hoplites had to be paid, and provisions bought. And large sums were demanded as ransom money for the release of prisoners of war. (According to Herodotus (V, 77), before the Persian invasion in the late sixth century the Athenians demanded two minas each for the release of Boeotian and Chalcidian prisoners.) In 480, when the Syracusans won a decisive victory over the Carthaginians at the Battle of Himera, Carthage paid an indemnity of 2,000 talents to Syracuse, and this vast amount of metal enabled the Syracusans to mint their own substantial coinage.

States also borrowed from the deities (i.e. from the temples), and some of the sums that the Athenians borrowed during the first years of the Peloponnesian War are preserved: an inscription found on the Acropolis records that between 433 and 426 they took 4,001 talents from Athena Polias and over 766 talents from the 'other gods'. The loans were made with an

Inscription listing expenses
of Athenian military
campaigns between 418
and 414 BC.
GR Inscriptions 23

interest rate of 1 drachm per day for every 5 talents, which is roughly 1.2 per cent a year. For only some loans are we told the exact purpose. For example, in 425 BC 30 talents were given to the general Demosthenes for use 'around the Peloponnese': this money was destined for Athenian operations at Pylos, a base which they had recently been established in Spartan territory. Another marble stele records loans from the treasury of Athena between 418 and 414 BC; here payments were granted to generals for various military operations (Meiggs, Lewis 77). It should be noted that payments did not have to be in Attic currency, as some were in electrum staters of Cyzicus.

Almost all the surviving evidence on this subject concerns the Peloponnesian War, whereas relatively little is known about finances and coinage during the Persian Wars. That money was spent during the years of the Persian invasions is clear from the large numbers of coins that were minted between 510 and 480. The Asyut hoard from Egypt, buried no earlier than 475, gives us an excellent picture of the coins that were produced in the period of the Persian Wars. Coins were minted in mainland Greece, the Aegean islands, Asia Minor, Lycia, Cyprus and Cyrenaeca, but in most cases they are not obviously associated with the war. Indeed, the locations of the hoards in which Greek coins appear during the first half of the fifth century suggest that hostilities between Greece and Persia did not prevent their circulation within the Persian empire.

What happens to coinage in the Peloponnesian War is better documented, and I have chosen the cases of Athens and the Peloponnesian League for particular discussion.

ATHENS

The tribute payments of the allies, together with the silver mines at Laurion in Attica, were the main sources of Athenian income in precious metal. Athens' considerable resources put her in a strong position at the outset of the war, as the Athenian statesman Perikles claims in a famous passage from Thucydides' *History of the Peloponnesian War* (II, XIII, 2-5):

The allies should be kept well in hand, for their power depended on the revenues which they derived from them; military successes were generally gained by a wise policy and command of money. The state of their finances was encouraging; they had on average 600 talents coming in annually from their allies, to say nothing of their other revenue; and there were still remaining in the Acropolis 6,000 talents of coined silver. (The whole amount had once been as much as 9,700 talents, but from this had to be deducted a sum of 3,700 expended on various buildings, such as the Propylaea of the Acropolis, and also on the siege of Potidaia.) Moreover there was uncoined gold and silver in the form of private and public offerings, sacred vessels used in processions and games, the Persian spoil and other things of like nature, worth at least 500 talents more. There were also at their disposal, besides what they had in the Acropolis, considerable treasures in various temples. If they were reduced to the last extremity they could even take off the plates of gold with which the image of the goddess was overlaid; these, as he pointed out, weighed forty talents, and were of refined gold, which was all removable. They might use these treasures in self-defence, but they were bound to replace all that they had taken.

This was written by Thucydides after Athens had lost the great war against Sparta, and some of the remarks attributed to Perikles are certainly influenced by subsequent events. As we saw above, the Athenian state borrowed heavily from their own temples, and this must have accelerated the minting of Athenian 'owls'; many of the so-called 'standardised owls', which look rather crude, may have been hurriedly minted during the early years of the war. By the early 420s, the financial pressure was starting to tell, and additional fund-raising measures had to be taken (see pp. 26-7). When in 415, however, the Athenians sent a large force to Sicily to support their allies Segesta and Leontini against Syracuse, Thucydides makes it clear that no expense was spared. Not only was this force wiped out, but on the home front the Spartans, on the advice of the renegade Athenian general Alkibiades, seized and fortified the village of Decelea in 413. This had a disastrous effect on the countryside of Attica: Thucydides says that over 20,000 slaves deserted. The mines of Laurion were soon brought to a standstill, and with them Athenian silver coinage. The Athenians tried to introduce a tax of 5 per cent on seaborne trade to replace the tribute payments from their allies, but enforcement seems to have been difficult and tribute was reimposed in 410. When Chios revolted in 412, the Athenians were driven to break into their iron reserve of 1,000 talents. This was money which had been set aside at the beginning of the war in 431 and which was to be used only when the city was attacked from the sea.

With the revolt of most of the allied cities in 412 and the loss of their mines, the situation became critical for the Athenians, and by 407/6 their silver reserves had been exhausted. Now the effect of the war on Athenian coinage can be clearly seen. The silver coinage ceased, and to meet payments in this crisis the Athenians removed the gold plate from the statues of Victory to mint their first gold coinage. Fourteen talents of gold were melted down, from which staters, drachms, diobols, obols and hemiobols were minted, bearing the same types as the silver coinage. The dies used for this coinage were kept in the treasury of Athena, where they are listed in a temple inventory of the fourth century: 'A wooden casket; a box in which the dies and the anvil are from which they struck the gold coins, sealed with the public seal' (*Inscriptiones graecae* , II^2, 1408). At the same time a bronze coinage was issued, to which the comic playwright Aristophanes twice refers. These were probably silver-plated, and it is today difficult to distinguish these wartime issues from later plated forgeries. With the defeat of the Athenians at the Battle of Aigospotamoi in 405 and the siege of Athens, Athenian coinage temporarily ceased altogether.

THE PELOPONNESIAN LEAGUE

Little is known about the financial resources of the Peloponnesian League, although like the Athenians it is said by Thucydides to have been at the height of its power when the Peloponnesian War started. The Spartans did not issue any coins until the Hellenistic period, but some of their allies did. The most important coinages in the Peloponnese were those of the Arkadian League and Elis. Some cities increased their minting activities during the war (Sikyon, which began to issue staters, Histiaia in northern Euboea, and some other Arkadian cities), but compared to Athens these coinages were on a very small scale. Even the coinage of Corinth is perhaps smaller than one would expect of this major international power.

Nevertheless, Sparta and her allies needed money if they were to challenge Athens at sea. Their main hope for financial help was the Persian king, and early in the war he was approached with requests for aid. We know that some of these attempts failed to reach him, and that the Peloponnesian envoys ended instead in Athenian hands. Thus in 425 the Athenians arrested a Persian in Eion in Thrace, who was carrying a letter destined for Sparta that was written in 'Assyrian script' (presumably Aramaic). This letter, when translated at Athens into Greek, was found to contain a complaint from the Persian king that he did not understand what the Spartans wanted and why they sent so many envoys. He asked them to send men back with the Persian envoy – an offer which the Athenians themselves then took up. What this episode shows is the hesitant approach of the Spartans towards Persia; this is hardly surprising, considering that they were claiming to fight for Greek freedom, while at the same time begging money from the man whose predecessors had tried to extinguish it! During the war in Ionia (after 412/11), the Spartans were less reluctant to use Persian help. At that stage, they had established their own fleet in the Aegean, and were employing mercenaries, many of whom came from Arkadia (for the involvement of the Persian satrap Tissaphernes and his payment in Attic money see p. 27).

Another example of how the war had a direct impact on coinage is provided by Corinth and some of her colonies. Corinth had been issuing coins in a regular series, but these were drastically reduced in 430 (though they perhaps did not cease altogether), when the Athenian naval blockade made Corinthian trade almost impossible. Like the island of Aegina, Corinth had no access to silver mines, which made coin production dependant on income from trade. It is disputed whether the coinage ceased altogether or continued on a very small scale (a few obverse dies survive), but it was in any case negligible. It has been argued that some rare issues that carry the Greek letter *epsilon* are to be attributed to their colony of Epidamnos in Illyria, and were minted to pay for military operations undertaken there shortly before the outbreak of war with Athens. Another issue of coins which appears to belong to a Corinthian colony carries an image of Pegasus with a horseman to which the letter *pi* has been added. These coins (see illustration, left) have been attributed to the Corinthian colony of Potidaia. Potidaia successfully appealed to the mother city Corinth for help against the besieging Athenians, and this coinage was perhaps used to pay the Corinthians who came to her aid.

The Corinthian colony of Potidaia probably minted this coin to pay for help in the war against the Athenians.
no.72

The general picture that emerges is that coined money became increasingly important for the effective waging of war in fifth-century Greece: Athens was brought down by lack of funds; Sparta only won when she had secured Persian financial backing. However, a city did not have to issue its own coinage in order to pay for war, and the case of Sparta shows that not all cities were impelled by civic pride to do so. Economic factors, such as the widespread acceptability of certain coins, transcended political boundaries. In other words, it did not much matter where money came from, provided only that it was available. It is a pleasing irony that the 'owls' of Athens, the city which lost the Peloponnesian War, were to become the international currency of the later Classical age.

Coinage and Athenian Society

O*wls from Laurion will never leave us;
but they will live within the city, and they will nest
in purses and carry off some small change.*
        ARISTOPHANES, *Birds*, 1106-8

Athens was a very wealthy city in the decades before the Peloponnesian War, and her citizens were proud of her. This pride was symbolised in her buildings, literature and sculptures, and also in her coins, referred to affectionately as 'owls' (see pp. 5-7). Coins are mentioned frequently in the comedies of Aristophanes, which suggests that they were commonly used by the average Athenian. Many citizens would have been paid in coins, and most would have spent them on a daily basis.

By 450 BC, Athenian jurors were paid 2 obols a day, increased to 3 obols in the 420s. These payments enabled everyone to perform his judicial duties as a citizen in a democratic society; for everyone was required to share the burden of administration, regardless of his income. Since many citizens lived outside the city of Athens in the outlying villages (demes) of Attica, attendance in the boulē (council) or in a jury could have often involved a day's walk into town; it was therefore a considerable sacrifice for someone who essentially lived off the produce of his land. By the middle of the fifth century, a large influx of foreigners into the city is evident: many were probably attracted by the life that Athens offered. Craftsmen were employed to work on the various building projects, and were paid in cash. Traders of foreign goods found an ideal market for their wares (see pp 12-13).

Rich Athenians seem to have kept some of their wealth at home in the form of coined money. For example, the orator

The Erechtheion, from which this graceful *kore* comes, was built during the Peloponnesian War and demonstrates the wealth and refinement of Athens at this period.
GR Sculpture 407

Lysias describes how he kept in a chest 'three talents of silver, four hundred Cyzicene staters, one hundred (Persian) darics, and four silver bowls' (Lysias 12, 11). The silver is exactly the sum that was paid in tribute to Athens by the rich city of Akanthos! Presumably the silver was in the form of Athenian tetradrachms rather than bullion. Others deposited it for safe-keeping with a banker. Although the operation of Athenian banks is best attested for the fourth century, they already existed in the late fifth. The security of banks was particularly useful for visiting traders, who had no safe place to keep their money.

How did a rich Athenian use his money? A certain amount was appropriated by the state. Although tribute from the empire cushioned Athenians from heavy taxes, the wealthiest were required to perform 'liturgies'. These were civic and military tasks, such as the fitting out of warships (*trierarchy*) or the sponsoring of choruses which competed at the dramatic festivals (*choregia*). All of the best-known works of Sophocles and Aristophanes were sponsored by wealthy backers. An element of competitive display can be discerned, as wealthy Athenians sought to gain prestige by outdoing their peers. Such sponsors could even be politically significant: in 472 the young Perikles won credit as the backer of Aeschylus' victorious play *The Persians*.

A more flamboyant use of wealth was made by Alkibiades, a flashy young aristocrat who rose to prominence in the last quarter of the fifth century. He spent lavishly on the expensive sport of chariot-racing. At the Olympic Games of 416, he entered no less than seven chariots, and came in first, second and fourth. Such expenditure was more typical of an Archaic tyrant, and was naturally regarded with suspicion by many of his compatriots; Alkibiades sought to justify it with the claim that it redounded to the credit of Athens.

Money was also spent in the service of the gods, both in Athens and beyond. An inscription records the fees payable by the initiates of the Mysteries at Eleusis in western Attica: 'The overseer to receive a hemiobol each day from each initiate. The

The greatest Greek statesman of the fifth century BC, Perikles (c. 495-429 BC) exerted a powerful influence over Athenian society and politics.
GR Sculpture 549

priest of Demeter is to receive at the Lesser Mysteries from each initiate an obol, and at the Greater Mysteries an obol from each initiate' (*Inscriptiones graecae,* I³, 6). Temples grew rich from the dedications that were made at them. Many of these were non-monetary, such as the numerous clay and bronze votive dedications at Olympia, although smaller items were no doubt purchased at the site by visitors to the sanctuary. The economy of this remote area of the Peloponnese was greatly boosted by the influx of people attending the Olympic Games; this is clear from its rich artistic treasures, and is also reflected in the series of beautiful coins issued by Elis, which carried a wide variety of images associated with Zeus' shrine. Temples also received coined money, as can be seen from numerous surviving Athenian financial records. For example, in an inscription of 405/4 the following offerings are listed: 'two gold Phocaean staters, twelve gold Phocaean *hektai*. Unsmelted gold, weight three and a half obols, ten silver Median *sigloi* … one gold Phocaean *hekte* … twelve bronze weights' (*Inscriptiones graecae,* I³, 342). A unique Aeginetan stater carries the inscribed graffito, 'To [the goddess] Matrobia, the sacred staters – ransom money'. Although the precise circumstances of this dedication are unclear, it is possible that the stater formed part of a ransom payment, and was later dedicated by a grateful devotee.

Temples were used to store both the equipment for coining, including even broken dies (see p. 34) and fake coins, which do not seem to have been destroyed. Does this indicate that coinage was regarded as somehow sacred – consider the image of Athena on Athenian coins – or was it that nobody had the authority to dispose of these items? We must at any rate avoid the modern assumption that God and Mammon should be kept apart. In the Greek world, the opposite seems to have been the case. Temples doubled as state treasuries and banks, and the Athenians had no qualms about using religious money for secular purposes – by the beginning of the Peloponnesian War, the treasurers of Athena were the main controllers of the Athenian reserve. Temple loans to individuals are attested at

Soldier in a Corinthian helmet depicted on the north frieze of the Parthenon.
GR North Frieze XXVII

Delos (Meiggs, Lewis 62) and at Rhamnous in Attica (Meiggs, Lewis 53). In the latter case the loans are all of either 200 or 300 drachms – clearly they were not adjusted to the different needs of each borrower.

The sums of money owned and spent by individuals were, however, trivial compared to those deployed by the state. As we have seen, vast amounts of coined money flowed into the Athenian treasuries every year. Much of this was spent on the fleet, but enough remained to pay for a series of massive building projects. The most famous is the Parthenon, the temple of Athena Parthenos, built to replace an earlier temple destroyed in the Persian sack of the city. Work started in 447/6, after peace with Persia had been made, and continued until 433/2. It has plausibly been argued that the total cost of the Parthenon, the cult statue of Athena and the Propylaea (the ceremonial gateway to the Acropolis) was of the order of 2,000 talents. At least 616 talents, but possibly as many as 1,000, were spent on Pheidias' famous colossal cult statue, which was made of gold and ivory. These buildings stood as a symbol of Athens' wealth and imperial power.

Athens' attitude to her empire was one of unapologetic domination: in Thucydides' *History of the Peloponnesian War*, Athenian speakers refer to their empire as a tyranny. At the city's festival of Dionysos, the year's tribute from the allies was paraded, talent by talent, in the theatre in front of the assembled crowds. We should imagine a procession of at least 400 men, each carrying 1,500 tetradrachms (over 50 pounds in weight). This display of wealth must have impressed not only the Athenians themselves but also any foreigners present. For the allies it was a galling sight. It was not surprising that Athens was confident of defeating Sparta, a city with no comparable buildings, coinage or fleet. But Athens was to meet her match at the hand of a far wealthier power – Persia. As Alexander the Great was to discover a century later, the treasuries of Persepolis and Ecbatana contained riches beyond the imagination of any Athenian.

Catalogue

All the coins listed here are illustrated actual size in the accompanying plates unless stated otherwise. The catalogue entries give the following information: the origin of the coin (usually a town or ruler); the location or other explanation of the coin's origin, and its date (all BC); brief descriptions of any images or impressions on the obverse and reverse; the British Museum registration or catalogue number, the metal from which the coin was made, some denominations and the coin's weight in grams. The following abbreviations have been used:

Metals

AR = *argentum* (silver), AE = *aes* (bronze), AV = *aurum* (gold), EL = electrum.

Bibliographical references

BMC = *A Catalogue of the Greek Coins in the British Museum*, London, 1873-1929; PCG = G.I. Hill, *A Guide to the Principal Coins of the Greeks*, London, 1932; SNG S.-C. = *Sylloge Nummorum Graecorum Great Britain*, vol. I, The Collection of Capt. E.G. Spencer-Churchill, London, 1931; SNG BM Black Sea = *Sylloge Nummorum Graecorum Great Britain*, vol. IX, British Museum, Pt 1: The Black Sea, London, 1993; SNG vA = *Sylloge Nummorum Graecorum Deutschland*, Sammlung von Aulock, Berlin, 1957-68; Starr = C.G. Starr, *Athenian Coinage, 480-449 BC*, Oxford, 1970.

1 Orescii
Thraco-Macedonian tribe, 480-460
Obv: man carrying two spears and leading two oxen, OPPHΣKION.
Rev: four-part incuse square.
BMC 2, AR, 28.13g.

2 Orescii
Thraco-Macedonian tribe, early 5th cent.
Obv: Centaur carrying off nymph.
Rev: four-part incuse square.
BMC 9, AR, 9.08g.

3 Neapolis
Macedonia, *c.* 500
Obv: Gorgoneion
Rev: four-part incuse square.
1931.4.10.18, AR, 7.27g.

4 Bisaltae
Thraco-Macedonian tribe, *c.* 470-60
Obv: man with two spears leading horse, BIΣAΛTIKΩN.
Rev: four-part incuse square.
BMC 2, AR, 27.43g.

5 Bisaltae
Thraco-Macedonian tribe, 470-60
Obv: man with two spears leading horse, BIΣAΛTIKΩN.
Rev: four-part incuse square.
1919.11.20.7, AR, octadrachm, 28.64g.

6 Getas
King of the Edones, *c.* 480-70
Obv: man with two oxen, ΝΟΜΙΣΜΑ ΕΔΟΝΕΟΝ ΒΑΣΙΛΕΟΣ ΓΙΤΑ ('coin of Getas, king of the Edones').
Rev: incuse with wheel.
1948.7.6.1, AR, 29.24g.

7 Laiai (?)
Thraco-Macedonian tribe, *c.* 480-470
Obv: man in chariot drawn by 2(?) oxen, helmet above, ΛΑΙΑΙ(?).
Rev: Pegasus in incuse.
BMC 2, AR, octadrachm, 32.08g.

8 Mosses
King of Bisaltae, 460-450
Obv: man with spear leading horse; helmet behind his back.
Rev: square incuse, ΜΟΣ ΣΕΩ around it.
1896.7.3.124, AR, 3.50g.

9 Akanthos
Macedonia, *c.* 480-70
Obv: bull attacked by lion, floral motif in exergue, O above.
Rev: four-part incuse square.
BMC 3, AR, tetradrachm, 17.04g.

10 Akanthos
Macedonia, *c.* 490-470
Obv: forepart of lion, floral decoration above.
Rev: four-part incuse square.
BMC 10, AR, tetrobol, 2.22g.

11 Akanthos
Macedonia, *c.* 490-470
Obv: head of Athena.
Rev: four-part incuse square.
BMC 16, AR, diobol, 1.23g.

12 Akanthos
Macedonia, *c.* 450
Obv: bull attacked by lion, grape in exergue, ΔΗ above lion.
Rev: incuse square, ΑΚΑΝΘΙΟΝ.
1896.6.1.16, AR, tetradrachm, 17.23g.

13 Akanthos
Macedonia, *c*. 400
Obv: bull attacked by lion,
ΑΛΕΞΙΟΣ in exergue.
Rev: incuse square, ΑΚΑΝΘΙΟΝ.
BMC 25, AR, tetradrachm, 14.29g.

14 Akanthos
Macedonia, *c*.400
Obv: bull with head turned back,
fish above.
Rev: four-part incuse square.
1958.3.4.20, AR, 2.26g.

15 Stageira
Macedonia, *c*. 500-490
Obv: boar attacked by lion.
Rev: four-part incuse square.
From a cast (SNG S-C 126)

16 Terone
Macedonia, *c*. 500-490
Obv: amphora.
Rev: four-part incuse square.
1971.5.13.4, AR, 14.09g.

17 Sermylia
Macedonia, *c*. 500-480
Obv: man on horse holding spear
above his head, ΣΕΡΜΥΛΙΑΟΝ.
Rev: four-part incuse square.
PCG IB 10, AR, 16.38g.

18 Aphytis
Macedonia, *c*. 450-440
Obv: bearded head with crested
helmet.
Rev: vine in shallow incuse, ΑΦΥΘ-
ΙΟΝ (last three letters retrograde)
around it.
1952.4.8.2, AR, 1.97g.

19 Skione
Macedonia, *c*. 480-460
Obv: male head.
Rev: dove, ΣΚΙΟ.
1981.9.15.16, AR, 1.83g.

20 Scione
Macedonia, *c*. 480-60
Obv: male head.
Rev: eye, ΣΚΙΟ.
1960.2.5.2, AR, 1.83g.

21 Mende
Thrace, *c*. 430
Obv: Dionysus on a donkey
holding a drinking cup.
Rev: vine in shallow incuse,
ΜΕΝΔΑΙΟΝ around it.
1940.10.1.3, AR, 16.93g.

22 Dikaia
Macedonia, *c*. 480-60
Obv: cock, octopus underneath it.
Rev: four-part incuse square.
1960.2.5.1, AR, 2.44g.

23 Dikaia
Macedonia, *c*. 480-60
Obv: cock, ΔΙ-ΚΑ.
Rev: shell
1986.4.24.12, AR, 0.68g.

24 Argilos
Macedonia, *c*. 500-480
Obv: Pegasus walking.
Rev: incuse square.
PGC IB 13, AR 13.61g.

25 Uncertain
Macedonia, *c*. 530-510
Obv: winged male figure running.
Rev: incuse square.
BMC 2, AR 7.42g.

26 Alexander I
King of Macedonia, *c*. 470-451
Obv: man with two spears walking
with horse.
Rev: incuse square, ΑΛΕΞΑΝΔΡΟΥ
around it.
BMC 3, AR, 25.44g.

27 Alexander I
King of Macedonia, *c*. 470-451
Obv: man on horse with two
spears.
Rev: forepart of goat, caduceus.
BMC 1, AR, 12.43g.

28 Bisaltae
Thracian tribe, *c*. 470-60
Obv: man walking with horse, bird
behind.
Rev: four-part incuse square.
1922.10.20.2, AR, 4.21g.

29 Perdikkas II
King of Macedonia, 451-413
Obv: man on horse holding two
spears.
Rev: forepart of lion, ΠΕΡ.
1919.11.20.57, AR 2.38g.

30 Perdikkas II
King of Macedonia, 451-413
Obv: man on horse, dog
underneath.
Rev: forepart of lion, caduceus.
BMC 25, AR, 2.31g.

31 Archelaos I
King of Macedonia, 413-399
Obv: man on horse holding two
spears.
Rev: forepart of goat, ΑΡΧΕΛΑΟ.
BMC 2, AR, 10.15g.

32 Archelaos I
King of Macedonia, 413-399
Obv: male head.
Rev: horse walking, ΑΡΧΕΛΑΟ.
BMC 2, AR, 10.15g.

33 Ainos
Thrace, *c*. 450-440
Obv: male head with helmet.
Rev: goat, wheel, AINI.
1890.5.3.1, AR, 16.55g.

34 Maroneia
Thrace, *c*. 430
Obv: horse running, male head
above, ΜΑΡΩΝΙΤΩΝ.
Rev: vine with four grapes,
ΜΗΤΡΟΔΟΤΟΣ.
1886.5.7.1, AR, 14.14g.

35 Dikaia
Thrace, *c.* 480-470
Obv: head of Herakles in lion's scalp.
Rev: bull's head, ΔIK.
BMC 3, AR, 7.29g.

36 Abdera
Thrace, *c.* 490-480
Obv: griffin with raised paw, ABΔH.
Rev: four-part incuse square.
1994.9.15.1, AR octadrachm, 29.80g.

37 Abdera
Thrace, *c.* 450
Obv: griffin, scarab beetle under raised paw.
Rev: four incuses, ΕΠΙ ΦΙΤΤΑΛΟ around them.
BMC 23, AR, 14.96g.

38 Abdera
Thrace, *c.* 430-420
Obv: griffin.
Rev: amphora, ΜΕΛΑΝΙΠΠΟΣ.
BMC 27, AR, 13.97g.

39 Thasos
Thracian island, *c.* 490-480
Obv: Satyr carrying off nymph.
Rev: four-part incuse square.
BMC 5, AR, 9.75g.

40 Thasos
Thracian island, *c.* 500-480
Obv: Satyr carrying off nymph.
Rev: four-part incuse square.
BMC 14, AR, 4.23g.

41 Thasos
Thracian island, *c.* 500-480
Obv: Satyr running.
Rev: four-part incuse square.
1994.7.17.1, AR, 1.15g.

42 Thasos
Thracian island, *c.* 500-480
Obv: two dolphins.
Rev: four-part incuse square.
BMC 21, AR, 0.46g.

43 Thasos
Thracian island, *c.* 500-480
Obv: one dolphin.
Rev: four-part incuse square.
BMC 23, AR, 0.30g.

44 Thasos
Thracian island, *c.* 430
Obv: satyr carrying off nymph.
Rev: four-part incuse square.
BMC 31b, AR, 3.70g.

45 Sparadokos
King of Thrace, *c.* 450-440
Obv: man on horse dressed in cloak and cap, with two long spears, helmet behind his back.
Rev: eagle picking up snake, ΣΠΑΡΑΔΟΚΟ around incuse square.
1890.5.4.2, AR, 16.96g.

46 Saratos (?)
Thracian King, end of 5th cent.
Obv: satyr running with drinking cup.
Rev: amphora, ΣΑΡ-ΑΤΟ.
BMC 1, AR, 1.13g.

47 Seuthes I
King of the Odrysae, late 5th cent.
Obv: man on horse.
Rev: ΣΕΥΘΑ ΚΟΜΜΑ (coin of Seuthes).
SNG BM Black Sea 315, AR, 9.59g.

48 Colchis
Black Sea, late 5th cent.
Obv: male head in round circle.
Rev: two heads in two incuse squares.
SNG BM Black Sea 1012, AR, 11.16g.

49 Delphi
c. 485-475
Obv: two ram's heads, two dolphins above, ΔΑΛΦΙΚΟΝ.
Rev: 'coffered ceiling' decorated with dolphins.
1971-5-13-1, AR, 18.40g.

50 Tanagra
c. 457-447
Obv: Boeotian shield.
Rev: forepart of horse, T-A.
BMC 23, AR, 11.87g.

51 Thebes
c. 426-395
Obv: Boeotian shield.
Rev: bearded head of Dionysus with ivy wreath.
BMC 60, AR, 12.21g.

52 Chalcis
Euboea, *c.* 500
Obv: man sitting on a horse.
Rev: four-part incuse.
1896-6-1-43, AR, 2.62g.

53 Eretria
Euboea, *c.* 405
Obv: female head, possibly of Euboea.
Rev: seated cow, vine grape above it, EYB.
1952.1.3.1, AR, 11.94g.

54 Athens
c. 510
Obv: head of Athena.
Rev: owl with olive sprig.
BMC 22, AR, 17.22g.

55 Athens
c. 479-475
Obv: head of Athena, four olive leaves on Attic helmet.
Rev: owl, olive twig with two leaves, small crescent, AΘE.
BMC 44, Starr I, no. 6., AR, tetradrachm, 17.18g.

56 Athens
c. 470
Obv: head of Athena, three olive leaves on Attic helmet.
Rev: owl, olive twig with two leaves, small crescent, AΘE.
BMC 73, Starr II B, no. 43, AR, didrachm, 8.22g.

57 Athens
c. 470
Obv: head of Athena, three olive leaves on Attic helmet.
Rev: owl, olive twig with two leaves, small crescent, AΘE.
1896.6.10.2, Starr II C, no. 64, AR, tetradrachm, 16.94g.

58 Athens
c. 470
Obv: head of Athena, three olive leaves on Attic helmet.
Rev: owl, olive twig with three leaves, small crescent, AΘE.
1922-10-20-31, Starr III, no. 95, AR, tetradrachm, 17.01g.

59 Athens
c. 465
Obv: head of Athena, three olive leaves on Attic helmet.
Rev: owl, olive twig with three leaves, small crescent, AΘE.
1949.4.11.421, Starr IV, no. 126, AR, 16.66g.

60-61 Athens
(original size and enlargement)
Second half of 5th cent.
Obv: head of Athena, three olive leaves on Attic helmet.
Rev: owl, olive twig with three leaves, small crescent, AΘE.
1949.4.11.462, AR, obol, 0.70g.

62-63 Athens
(original size and enlargement)
Second half of 5th cent.
Obv: head of Athena, three olive leaves on Attic helmet.
Rev: owl, olive twig with three leaves, small crescent, AΘE.

1920. 8.5.364, AR, hemiobol, 0.31g.

64 Athens
'Standardised type', second half of 5th cent.
Obv: head of Athena, three olive leaves on Attic helmet.
Rev: owl, olive twig with three leaves, small crescent, AΘE.
1967.8.8.9, AR, 17.22g.

65 Athens
Second half of 5th cent.
Obv: head of Athena, three olive leaves on Attic helmet.
Rev: owl, olive twig with three leaves, small crescent, AΘE.
1920.8.5.328, AR, drachm, 4.29g.

66 Athens
Second half of 5th cent.
Obv: head of Athena.
Rev: facing owl, olive sprig.
BMC 86, AR, triobol, 2.11g.

67 Athens
c. 405
Obv: head of Athena, three olive leaves on Attic helmet.
Rev: owl, olive twig with three leaves, small crescent, AΘE.
PCG Add. 17, AV, stater, 8.59g.

68 Athens
c. 405
Obv: head of Athena
Rev: facing owl, olive sprig.
PCG, II.B.36, AV, quarter-stater, 2.16g.

69 Athens
Bronze money, *c.* 405
Obv: head of Athena, three olive leaves on Attic helmet.
Rev: owl, olive twig with three leaves, small crescent, AΘE.
BMC 61, plated bronze, 14.85g.

70 Athens
Imitation from Egypt in rather crude style, 4th cent.
Obv: head of Athena.
Rev: owl.
1937.11.6.5, AR, 17.10 g.

71 Athens
4th cent. type
Obv: head of Athena.
Rev: owl.
1924.1.14.1, AR, 17.15g.

72 Corinthian colony, possibly Potidaia
c. 432-1
Obv: Pegasus with a man on it, P below.
Rev: head of Athena, Π behind the head.
1952.12.1.1, AR, 8.61g

73 Aegina
Aegean island, *c.* 475-465
Obv: turtle with T-shape back.
Rev: incuse square with pattern.
BMC 95, AR, 12.27g.

74 Pseudo-Aegina
Imitation, *c.* 520-500
Obv: turtle.
Rev: incuse.
1914.6.7.9, AR, 11.93g.

75 Pseudo-Aegina
Possibly Egyptian imitation of Attic weight, first half of 5th cent.
Obv: turtle.
Rev: incuse.
1921-6-13-1, AR, 16.85g.

76 Aegina
Aegean island, *c.* 445 (?)
Obv: tortoise.
Rev: incuse with pattern.
BMC 147, AR, 12.37g.

77 Corinth
Peloponnese, *c.* 470
Obv: Pegasus, letter *koppa* below it.
Rev: head of Athena in Corinthian helmet.
1953.5.6.8, AR, 8.56g.

78 Sikyon
Peloponnese, *c.* 480
Obv: dove flying.
Rev: letter *sigma* in incuse.
1949.4.11.633, AR, 5.76g.

79 Argos
Peloponnese, *c.* 450
Obv: forepart of wolf.
Rev: A in incuse.
BMC 13, AR, 2.91g.

80 Arkadian League
c. 460-50
Obv: seated figure of Zeus.
Rev: head of Aphrodite, ΑΡΚΑΔΙΚΟΝ.
BMC 33, AR, 2.93g.

81 Arkadian League
c. 450
Obv: seated figure of Zeus.
Rev: head of Aphrodite, ΑΡΚΑΔΙΚΟΝ.
BMC 42, AR, 2.89g.

82 Elis
Peloponnese, *c.* 430
Obv: eagle attacking hare.
Rev: thunderbolt, F - A.
BMC 19, AR, 12.14g.

83 Elis
Peloponnese, *c.* 460
Obv: eagle attacking hare.
Rev: winged female figure (Nike), Φ - A.
BMC 10, AR, 11.93g.

84 Crete, Pseudo-Aegina
First half of 5th cent.
Obv: turtle, crescent to left.
Rev: incuse with pattern.
BMC 113, AR, 3.36g.

85 Kyzikos
Mysia, second half of 5th cent.
Obv: dog.
Rev: four-part incuse square.
1914.11.3.1, EL, 16.22g.

86 Kyzikos
Mysia, second half of 5th cent.
Obv: naked man with Corinthian helmet testing an arrow, his bow in front, tunny fish.
Rev: four-part incuse square.
BMC 79, EL, 16.00g.

87 Parion
Mysia, first half of 5th cent.
Obv: Gorgoneion.
Rev: cross-shaped incuse.
1949.4.1.715, AR, 3.26g.

88 Abydos (enlargement)
c. 470-450
Obv: eagle, ABYΔ.
Rev: Gorgoneion.
1979.1.1.248, SNG vA 7532, AR, 5.23g.

89 Kyme
c. 470-450
Obv: head of eagle.
Rev: incuse square.
1979.1.1.305, AR, 1.19g.

90 Kyme
c. 460-450
Obv: head of horse.
Rev: incuse square.
1979.1.1.307, SNG vA 1622, AR, 0.91g.

91 Klazomenai
c. 500
Obv: winged boar forepart.
Rev: incuse square.
BMC 6, AR, 6.98g.

92 Ephesos
c. 480-470
Obv: bee.
Rev: four-part incuse square.
BMC 8, AR, 3.20g.

93 Erythrai
c. 460
Obv: man leading horse.
Rev: flower in incuse square.
BMC 29, AR, 4.60g.

94 Magnesia, Themistocles
Ionia, *c.* 465
Obv: Apollo standing.
Rev: eagle, MA.
BMC 1, plated, 5.84g.

95 Teos (enlargement)
Ionia, *c.* 450-40
Obv: griffin, THION.
Rev: four-part incuse square.
This coin is overstruck on a coin of Aegina (cf. no. 76).
1988.6.5.1, AR, 11.95g.

96 Persian satrapal issue
c. 420
Obv: head of a Persian satrap in tiara.
Rev: owl, with olive sprig and crescent, ΒΑΣ (which stands for 'of the King' of Persia).
1947.7.6.4, AR, 16.69g.

97 Astyra (enlargement)
c. 400-395
Obv: head of bearded Tissaphernes, ΤΙΣΣΑ underneath head.
Rev: statue of female goddess, ΑΣΤΥΡΑ.
1994.7.18.1, AE, 1.48g.

98 Chios
Aegean island, *c.* 440 (?)
Obv: sphinx, sitting in front of an amphora, grapes above.
Rev: four-part incuse square.
BMC 17, AR, 3.64g.

99 Samos
Aegean island, *c.* 450
Obv: frontal lion scalp.
Rev: forepart of a bull, olive sprig, ΣΑ.
BMC 90, AR, 12.86g.

100 Knidos
Aegean island, *c.* 460
Obv: lion's forepart.
Rev: head of Aphrodite, KNI.
1918.2.4.140, AR, 6.07g.

101 Knidos
Aegean island, *c.* 430
Obv: lion's forepart right.
Rev: head of Aphrodite.
1926.2.3.8, AR, 6.13g.

102 Caria
Uncertain mint, *c.* 510-500
Obv: head of sea monster.
Rev: incuse square with dots.
1979.1.1.474, SNG vA 8035, AR,
1.69g.

103 Histiaeus
Tyrant of Termera, Caria, *c.* 490-80
Obv: lion head, leg below.
Rev: Man fighting lion, ΙΣΤΙΑΙ-Ο.
1980.11.24.1, AR, 4.58g.

104 Tymnes, Termera
Tyrant of Termera, Caria, after 480
Obv: Heracles, TYMNO.
Rev: lion's head, ΤΕΡΜΕΡΙΚΟΝ.
BMC 2, AR, 4.69g.

105 Kalymna
Caria, *c.* 500
Obv: helmeted head.
Rev: lyre.
BMC 2, AR, 10.51g.

106 Kos
Aegean Island, *c.* 480-470
Obv: discus-thrower, tripod, ΚΩΣ.
Rev: crab in incuse square.
BMC 8, AR, 16.58g.

107 Ialysos
City on Rhodes, *c.* 500-480
Obv: Winged boar forepart,
ΙΑΛΥΣΙΟΝ.
Rev: Head of eagle in incuse
square, ΙΑΛΥΣΙΟΝ.
BMC 3, AR, 14.47g.

108 Kamiros
City on Rhodes, *c.* 460
Obv: fig-leaf.
Rev: KAMI-ΡΕΩΝ in incuse.
BMC 12, AR, 11.33g.

109 Lycia
Teththiveibi, dynast, 440 BC
Obv: female head (Aphrodite?).
Rev: owl, Teththiveibi in Lycian
script.
1934.6.1.3, AR, 9.64g.

110 Lycia
Tênagure, dynast, *c.* 440
Obv: winged and horned lion,
symbol.
Rev: trisceles, symbol repeated
twice.
BMC 83, AR, 8.50g.

111 Lycia
Vekhssere, dynast, *c.* 390
Obv: forepart of lion, above N-E.
Rev: facing head of Athena,
Vekhssere in Lycian script.
1964.2.15.12, AR, 9.68g.

112 Aspendos
Pamphylia, *c.* 480-460
Obv: helmeted warrior with shield.
Rev: trisceles, ΕΣΤFΕ.
1979.1.1.844, SNG vA 4480, 10.79g.

113 Aspendos
Pamphylia, *c.* 420-360 BC
Obv: man on horse.
Rev: boar, countermark.
1979.1.1. 849 SNG vA 4495, 5.38g

114 Aspendos
Pamphylia, *c.* 420-360
Obv: man on horse.
Rev: boar (to left) with six different
countermarks
1909.5.2.25, AR, 5.20g

115 Side
Pamphylia, *c.* 460
Obv: pomegranate, dolphin.
Rev: head of Athena.
BMC 2, AR, 10.96g.

116 Kelenderis
Pamphylia, *c.* 420
Obv: man on horse.
Rev: goat, ΚΕΛ.
1979.1.1.965, SNG vA 5624, AR,
10.79g.

117 Paphos
Stasandros, king of Cyprus,
c. 440-420
Obv: bull, winged solar disc above,
ankh sign.
Rev: eagle, vase, βασι Σα-τα-σα (in
Cypriote script).
BMC 13, AR, 10.92g.

118 Citium
Baalmek II, king, Cyprus,
c. 425-400
Obv: Herakles with bow and club.
Rev: lion attacking stag, name of
king in Aramaic script.
BMC 35, AR, 10.98g.

119 Persia (enlargement)
Fourth century
Obv: Persian king with bow.
Rev: rough incuse.
1993.9.21.2, AR, 5.20g.

120 Persia (enlargement)
4th cent.
Obv: Persian king with bow and
dagger.
Rev: rough incuse.
1993.9.21.1, AR, 5.51g.

121 Cyrene
510-480
Obv: silphium plant.
Rev: lion bringing down prey (seen
from above).
1971. 5.13.12, AR, 17.27g.

1

2

3

4

5

6

7   8   9   10

11   12   13   14

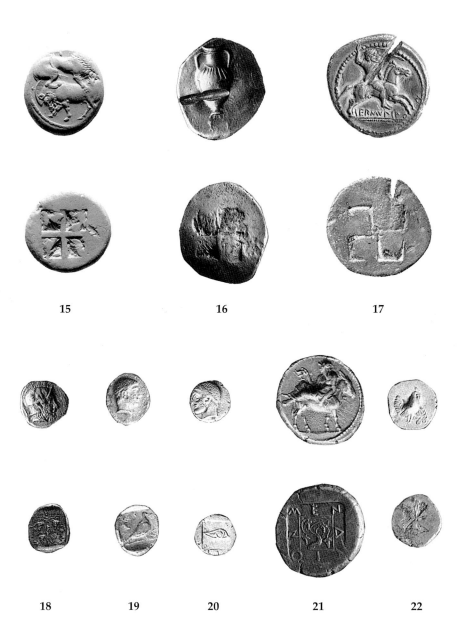

15   16   17

18   19   20   21   22

23   24   25   26

27   28   29   30

31   32   33   34

35   36   37   38

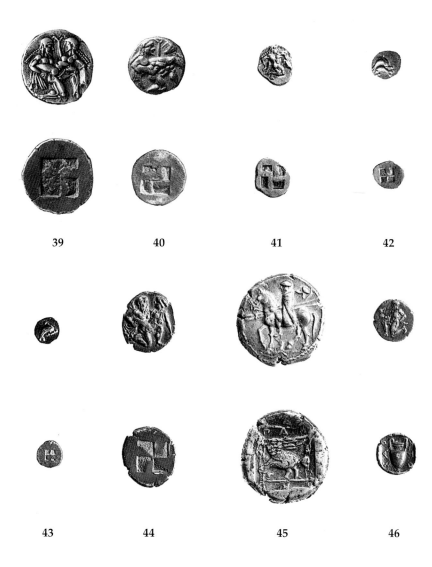

39   40   41   42

43   44   45   46

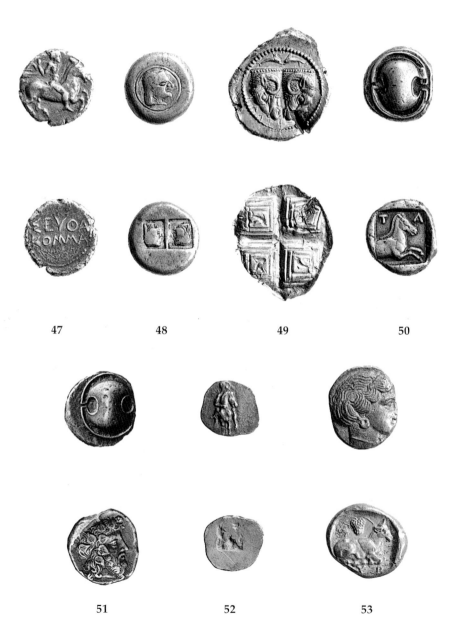

47   48   49   50

51   52   53

54   55   56   57

58   59   60   61

62   63   64   65   66

67   68   69   70   71

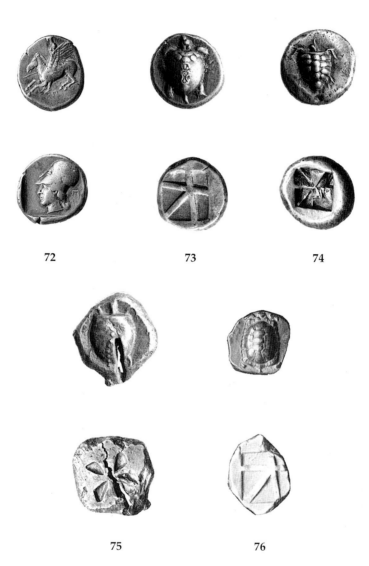

72   73   74

75   76

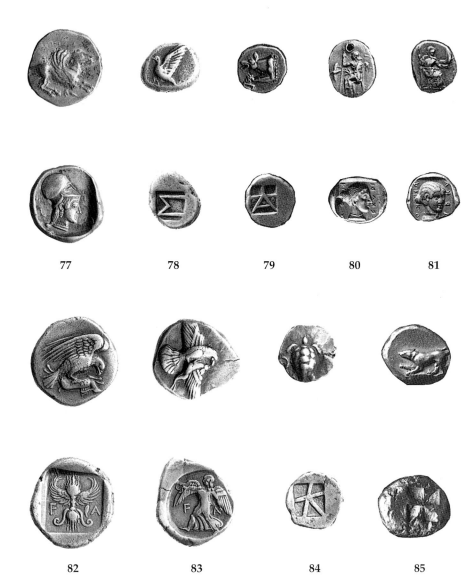

77   78   79   80   81

82   83   84   85

86   87   89   90

88

91   92   93   94

95

96 97 98 99

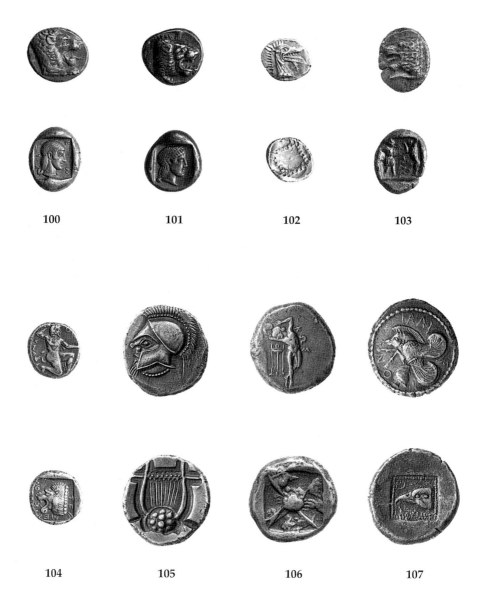

100   101   102   103

104   105   106   107

108   109   110   111

112   113

114

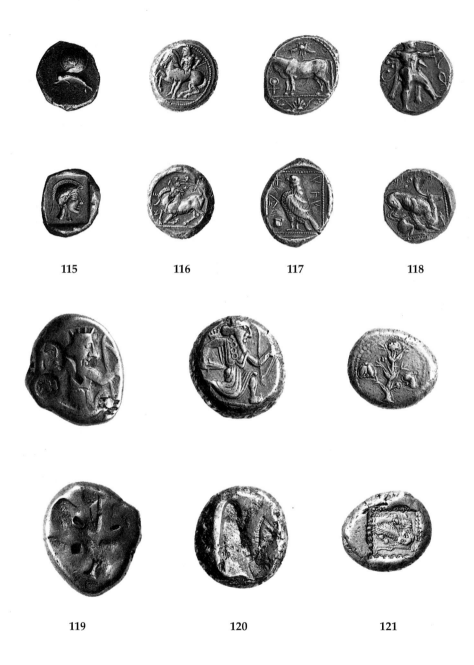

115   116   117   118

119   120   121

N.G. ASHTON, 'What does the turtle say?', *Numismatic Chronicle* 1987, 1-7.

E. BOEHRINGER, *Die Münzen von Syrakus*, Berlin, 1929.

H. A. CAHN, 'Tissaphernes in Astyra', *Archäologischer Anzeiger* (1985), 587-594.

H. A. CAHN, 'Dynast oder Sartrap?', *Schweizer Münzblätter* 25 (1975), 84-91.

H.A. CAHN, 'Stagira in Tel-Aviv', *Studies in honor of Leo Mildenberg*, ed. A. Houghton et al. Wetteren, 1984, 43-50.

I. CARRADICE, M. PRICE, *Coinage in the Greek World*, London, 1988.

I. CARRADICE, 'The 'regal' coinage of the Persian Empire', in: I. Carradice et al., *Coinage and administration in the Athenian and Persian Empire*, 9th symposium on Coinage and Monetary History, (BAR 343, 1987), pp. 73-95.

M. CHAMBERS, R. GALLUCCI, P. SPANOS, 'Athens' Alliance with Egesta in the year of Antiphon', Zeitschrift für Papyrologie und Epigraphik 83 (1990), 38-63.

Coin Hoards I-VIII, London, 1975-1994.

J. DESNEUX, 'Les tétradrachms d'Akanthos', *Revue belge numismatique* 90 (1949), pp. 5-122.

E. ERXLEBEN, 'Das Münzgesetz des delisch-attischen Seebundes, II. Die Münzen', '- III, Die Datierung', *Archiv für Papyrusforschung* 20 (1970), pp. 66-132; 21 (1971), pp. 145-162.

S. FRIED, 'The Decadrachm hoard: an introduction', in: *Coinage and administration in the Athenian and Persian Empire*, pp. 1-10.

Inventory of Greek Coin Hoards, ed. M. Thompson, O. Mørkholm, C.M. Kraay, New York, 1973.

G.K. JENKINS, *Greek Coins*, 2nd ed., London, 1983.

C. HEIPP-TAMER, *Die Münzprägung der lykischen Stadt Phaselis in griechischer Zeit*. (Saarbrücker Studien zur Archäologie und Alten Geschichte, vol. 6), Saarbrücken, 1993.

S. HURTER, 'Teos over Tanagra', *Florilegium Numismaticum. Studia in honorem U. Westermark edita*, Stockholm, 1992, 171-173.

J.H. KAGAN, 'The Decadrachm hoard: chronology and consequences', in: *Coinage and administration in the Athenian and Persian Empire*, pp. 21-28,

L. KALLET-MARX, *Money, Expense, and Naval Power in Thucydides' History 1-5.24*, Berkeley, 1993.

C.M. KRAAY, *Archaic and Classical Greek Coins*, London, 1976.

C.M. KRAAY, 'The Coinage of Ambracia and the the Preliminaries of the Peloponnesian War', *QT* 8 (1979), 37-59.

D.M. LEWIS, 'The Athenian Coinage Decree', *Coinage and administration in the Athenian and Persian Empire*, pp. 53-63.

K. LIAMPI, 'Argilos. History and Coinage. *Nomimatika Khronika* 13 (1994), 7-36.

J.M.F. MAY, *The Coinage of Abdera*, London, 1966.

D. MCDONALD, 'A Teos/Abdera overstrike', *SM* 44, 174 (Sept. 1994), 37-40.

H. B. MATTINGLY, 'The Athenian Coinage Decree and the assertion of Empire', *Coinage and administration in the Athenian and Persian Empire*, 65-71.

H.B. MATTINGLY, 'A new light on the early silver coinage of Teos', *Schweizer Numismatische Rundschau* 73 (1994), 5-9.

O. PICARD, 'Monnayage thasien du Ve siècle av. Jésus-Christ', *Académie des inscriptions & Belles-Lettres, Comptes Rendues* (July-Oct., 1982), 412-424

R. MEIGGS, D.M. LEWIS, *Greek Historical Inscriptions*, Oxford, 1969

L. MILDENBERG, 'Über das Münzwesen im Reich der Achämeniden', *Archäologische Mitteilungen aus Iran* 26 (1993), 55-79.

M.J. PRICE, 'The coinages of the Northern Aegean', *Coinage and administration in the Athenian and Persian Empire*, 43-47.

M.J. PRICE, N. Waggoner, *Archaic Greek Silver Coinage: the Asyut Hoard*, London 1975.

M.J. PRICE, 'Histiaeus, son of Tymnes, tyrant of Termera, Caria', *Norwegian Numismatic Journal* Sept. 1979, 8-12.

M.D.RAYMOND, *Macedonian Regal Coinage to 413 B.C.*, Numismatic Notes and Monographs 126, New York, 1953.

E.S.G. ROBINSON, 'Pseudoaeginetica', *Numismatic Chronicle* 1928, 172-198.

E.S.G. ROBINSON, 'Some problems in the later fifth century coinage of Athens', *American Numismatic Society Museum Notes* 9 (1960), 1-15.

B. A. SPARKES, *Greek Pottery, An Introduction*. Manchester, 1991.

J. SPIER, 'Emblems in Archaic Greece', *Bulletin of the Institute for Classical Studies* 37 (1990), 107-129.

J. SPIER, 'Lycian coins in the Decadrachm hoard', *Coinage and administration in the Athenian and Persian Empire*, 29-37.

C.G. STARR, *Athenian Coinage 480-449 B.C.*, Oxford, 1970.

Y. YOUROUKOVA, *Coins of the Ancient Thracians*, BAR Suppl. 4, Oxford, 1976.

Index of Coins